NICOTEXT

Never have I ever – Dirty

NICOTEXT part of Cladd media ltd.
www.nicotext.com
info@nicotext.com

Printed in Poland
ISBN: 978-91-86283-84-1

DO NOT DRINK AND DRIVE & DO NOT DRINK ALCOHOL IF YOU ARE UNDER DRINKING AGE!

...AND KIDS, REMEMBER, ALWAYS WEAR A CONDOM!

- Gather all your friends in a circle.

- Decide on a tell. It could be to raise your pinky, stand straight up, put a coin on the table or take a sip of your drink. All the players must use the same tell.

- Decide if you're going to use the red or the black statements (They're both just as horrible).

- The naughtiest person in the room opens the book at random and reads the statement out loud.

- If the statement is true (for example: "Never Have I Ever had erotic fantasies about a character from the Simpsons."), you don't have to do anything. But if it's false (for example:

"Never Have I Ever wiped my ass with granny's underwear.") you have to show your tell. All players do this at the same time.

- After each statement, pass the book clockwise.

- If someone picks the exact same statement, simply choose a new page.

BONUS: If a person has the luck to confess three times in a row, the player on his/her right may ask him/her one revealing question in the same subject.

Never have

Never have I ever had groupsex.

Never have I ever been unfaithful
to a partner.

Never have

Never have I ever had sex in public.

Never have I ever fantasized
about animals.

Never have

Never have I ever had anal sex.

Never have I ever had an STD.

Never have I ever had sex with more than one person in a 24-hour period.

Never have I ever stopped having sex
because someone was seriously hurt.

I ever

Never have

Never have I ever **lied** just to get sex.

Never have I ever screamed the wrong name during sex.

Never have I ever taken
someone's virginity.

Never have I ever had more
than ten orgasms in a day.

Never have

Never have I ever stolen my lover's underwear.

Never have I ever fantasized
about BDSM.

Never have I ever had sex with a person without knowing their name.

Never have I ever used a glory hole.

Never have I ever been to
a nudist beach.

Never have I ever spread an STD.

Never have I ever had sex
with someone in this room.

Never have I ever masturbated in public.

Never have

Never have I ever used a
vegetable as a sex toy.

Never have I ever taken the morning after pill/made someone take the morning after pill.

Never have I ever had sex
while watching a porno.

Never have I ever played
S & M games.

Never have I ever had
sex at a party.

Never have I ever watched a snuff movie.

Never have I ever lied about
how many I've slept with.

Never have I ever worn certain
clothes only to hide a hickey.

Never have

Never have I ever had sex
with a famous person.

Never have I ever fallen
asleep during sex.

Never have I ever had sex
in my parent's bed.

Never have I ever had sex on public transportation.

Never have I ever experienced a sexual dream about a relative.

Never have I ever had sex on a beach.

Never have I ever faked
an orgasm.

Never have I ever had sex
with someone more than 15
years older than me.

Never have I ever had sex even
if I didn't really want to.

Never have I ever tasted cum.

Never have I ever gotten sexual
advice from my parents.

Never have I ever had a threesome.

Never have I ever snuck away from
a one-night-stand without
saying goodbye.

Never have I ever burped on someone
I was kissing at the time.

Never have

Never have I ever found a sexual partner on the Internet.

Never have I ever used a sex
toy on a partner.

Never have I ever had sex at work.

Never have I ever stayed home from work/school just to have sex.

Never have I ever licked someone's ass
(anallingus).

Never have I ever had sex
in a sleeping bag.

Never have I ever sent naked
pictures to a lover.

Never have I ever watched
animal porn.

Never have I ever had sex on
an airplane.

Never have I ever tasted my own genitals.

Never have

Never have I ever swallowed
sexual juices.

Never have I ever had
sex in a car.

Never have I ever had so much sex that I couldn't walk properly.

Never have I ever had sex with
my friend's partner.

Never have I ever been to a
swingers party.

Never have I ever paid someone for sex/been paid for sex.

Never have I ever done the
"walk of shame".

Never have I ever experienced
a golden shower.

Never have I ever been so intoxicated
that I've forgot that I've had sex.

Never have I ever done the

69.

Never have I ever turned off the light during sex because I was feeling uncomfortable.

Never have I ever been
to a strip club.

Never have I ever posed naked
on the Internet.

Never have I ever had unsafe
sex on purpose.

Never have I ever shaved my
intimate parts completely.

Never have I ever
cried during sex.

Never have I ever starred in a
home pornographic video.

Never have I ever had
sex on a toilet.

Never have I ever had sex for more than 3 hours straight.

Never have I ever had sex during my period/when my partner had her period.

Never have

Never have I ever used sex toys
during sex with someone.

Never have I ever gotten
spanked/spanked someone.

Never have

Never have I ever had
trouble getting off.

Never have I ever had sex
against a washing machine.

Never have I ever been so drunk
that I peed my own bed.

Never have I ever had
sex on a roof.

Never have I ever been
strangled during sex.

Never have I ever had sex while
driving a car (you or your partner).

Never have I ever experienced
foot fetishism.

Never have I ever thrown my underwear
on stage at a concert.

Never have I ever lost a bet so that
I had to give someone sex.

Never have I ever …
you decide!

Never have I ever had sex
against a wall.

Never have I ever tasted my own juices.

Never have I ever had sex to the rhythm of music.

Never have I ever experienced
a titty fuck.

Never have I ever had sex
with a colleague.

Never have I ever listened to other people having sex.

Never have I ever had sex without kissing my partner on the mouth.

Never have I ever had sex
in a public pool.

Never have

Never have I ever had sex while pregnant or with a pregnant woman.

Never have I ever experienced
squirting.

Never have I ever slapped my partner.

Never have I ever been
fisted/fisted someone.

Never have I ever choked
on a pubic hair.

Never have I ever given someone
a lap dance/gotten a lap dance.

Never have I ever swopped partners
with a friend just for sex.

Never have I ever felt disgusted
during sex.

Never have

Never have I ever had sex with someone just because I knew my friend was interested in that person.

Never have I ever stopped having
sex just to answer the phone.

Never have I ever put a sex tape
on the Internet.

Never have I ever watched myself
cum in a mirror or on video.

Never have I ever role-played with costumes.

Never have I ever woken up
to someone giving me oral sex.

Never have I ever had sex in
a dressing room.

Never have I ever had sex with
my boss or teacher.

Never have I ever vomited during sex.

Never have I ever made obscene phone calls just to get off.

Never have I ever felt like I never
want to have sex again.

Never have I ever talked
someone in to having sex.

Never have I ever had sexual fantasies
about having sex with a dead person.

Never have I ever had complains about me being too loud during sex.

Never have I ever farted during sex.

Never have I ever worn fetish clothes during sex.

Never have I ever watched
someone else having sex.

Never have I ever smelt
someone's underwear.

Never have I ever peed
myself during sex.

Never have I ever **streaked**.

Never have I ever been
blindfolded during sex.

Never have I ever had sex
at a funeral.

Never have I ever
flashed someone.

Never have I ever had sex
in a club/bar.

Never have I ever accidently told someone I love them just because the sex was so good.

Never have I ever shaved my partner's intimate parts.

Never have I ever had sex in a hospital.

Never have I ever been to a sex party.

Never have I ever had sex
while being high.

Never have I ever had
sex at a festival.

Never have I ever ridden
someone’s face.

Never have I ever had interrupted sex as a method of birth control.

Never have I ever been aggressive in bed.

Never have I ever had sex
with my socks on.

Never have I ever had sex
in a movie theatre.

Never have I ever had sex with someone more than 10 years younger than myself.

Never have

Never have I ever fallen in love
with a one-night-stand.

Never have I ever bragged about
how many I've slept with.

Never have I ever experienced
a strap-on.

Never have I ever made a booty call.

Never have I ever had sex
with a friend's parent.

Never have I ever been tied
up during sex.

Never have I ever spent a whole day watching porn and masturbating.

Never have I ever regretted having sex with someone.

Never have I ever had sex outside
in the winter.

Never have I ever been in a relationship
with a sex fanatic.

Never have I ever had a “perfect week”
(sex with a different person every
day for 7 days straight).

Never have I ever stopped having
sex just to laugh about it.

Never have

Never have I ever changed my mind
about having sex when I saw
the person naked.

Never have I ever had painful sex.

Never have I ever spat in someone's
face during sex.

Never have I ever talked
dirty during sex.

Never have I ever had sex in the same room where others were sleeping.

Never have I ever had sex in order
to get a job or other benefits.

Never have I ever experienced
pierced genitals.

Never have I ever had sex
over webcam.

Never have I ever been a groupie.

Never have I ever been accused
of being a sex addict.

Never have I ever swopped partners.

Never have I ever used
a **butt** plug.

Never have I ever had sex with
someone that was married
to someone else.

Never have I ever had
sex on a table.

Never have I ever slept
on the wet spot.

Never have I ever fantasized about another person while having sex with my partner.

Never have I ever been passive in bed.

Never have I ever denied that
I had sex with someone.

Never have I ever pleased someone else
sexually without getting off myself.

Never have I ever had sex on
the hood of a car.

Never have

Never have I ever used electrical stimulation during sex.

Never have I ever had sex on a bus.

Never have I ever taught someone
to perform something sexual.

Never have I ever ...
you decide!

Never have I ever had sex on a stage.

Never have I ever smeared sexual juices on a piece of furniture.

Never have I ever been without sex
for more than six months.

Never have I ever had sex with
a MILF or a DILF.

Never have I ever made my
partner have sex with me.

Never have I ever gotten inspired by
a porno to try new sexual things.

Never have I ever had an “air-orgasm” (an orgasm without any physical stimulation).

Never have I ever used a bad excuse
just to get out of having sex
(like headache).

Never have

Never have I ever wished that I had waited longer with loosing my virginity.

Never have I ever told someone that
the sex was great when it
was awful.

Never have I ever had a sexual injury
that I had to seek help for.

Never have I ever had a hickey
on my intimate parts.

I ever

Never have I ever been in an open relationship.

Never have I ever asked a friend to have sex with me just because I couldn't get it anywhere else.

Never have I ever had oil sex.

Never have I ever started a fight
just to get **make-up** sex.

Never have I ever gone out to
a bar just to get sex.

Never have I ever been too drunk
to perform sexually.

Never have I ever lied while playing
Never have I ever.

Never have I ever written a list with reviews of my sexual partners.

Never have I ever had hot candle wax dripped over my body during sex.

Never have I ever masturbated to
the sound of my neighbours
having sex.

Never have I ever experienced
edible underwear.

Never have I ever had sex more
than five times in one day.

Never have I ever had sex on a boat.

Never have I ever bitten someone's genitalia, **hard**.

Never have I ever had sex outdoors.

Never have I ever
been in love.